Rhyme of the Week

Anne Linehan
and
Jennifer Kaplan

A Teaching Resource Center Publication

Published by
Teaching Resource Center
P.O. Box 82777
San Diego, CA 92138

Edited by Laura Woodard
Design and production by Janis Poe
Illustrations by Linda Starr

Printed in the United States of America
ISBN: 1-56785-043-X

Acknowledgments

Thank you to Cynthia Christian who generously shared her students. And to Mary McMahon, a special friend and great teacher who gave her time and expertise. A special thanks to those students that helped me understand the best elements of the lessons: Alejandra, Alfonso, Jesús, Jose, Luis, Omar, Sameer, and Vanessa of Baywood School in San Mateo, California.

Anne Linehan

This book is dedicated to my nieces and nephews Holland, Julika, Benjamin, Amanda, Briana and Jared. A heartfelt thanks to Anne for providing the opportunity to collaborate with her on this book and for being especially patient while I attended graduate school across the country.

Jennifer Kaplan

Choosing Rhymes

To help you select the rhyme that best fits your curriculum needs, we have organized them in two ways:

1. The rhymes are alphabetized by title in the table of contents.

2. In the chart on page 3, the rhymes have been organized by possible classroom teaching themes and by curriculum focus.

Table of Contents

Curriculum and Theme Ideas for the Rhymes — Reading — Math

Many of the rhymes have multiple uses and appear a number of times.

Reading — sight words (repeats at least twice in the poem)
Math — number words, mathematics

Rhyme	name	food	animals	colors	music	geography	science	movement	opposites	first letter	rhyming	rimes, chunks	sight words	number words	mathematics	page
A My Name is Alice	■	■		■	■			■	■				is, my			11
Baa, Baa, Black Sheep			■	■									the, yes, and, for	■	one to one	12
Cat and the Fiddle, The			■		■		■	■					the, and			13
Cinderella				■				■					a		rote counting	14
Days in the Month							■						and	■	calendar	15
Duke of York, The								■	■				he, the, up, and, down	■	large numbers	16
Elephants on a Web			■				■	■				-ay	she, to		one more	49
Five Speckled Frogs			■	■										■	one less	50
Fuzzy Wuzzy			■											■		17
Hickory, Dickory, Dock			■		■			■					the	■	time	18
Higglety, Pigglety			■									-op	the, in, a			19
Hush, Little Baby			■									-ing, -ass, -ay	if, the, to, a, you			20
Ice Cream Soda		■						■								21
Itsy, Bitsy Spider, The			■				■	■					and, the, up		size	22
It's Raining							■	■				-ing	and, the, It's			23
Jack and Jill	■							■				-ill	and			24
Lady With the Alligator Purse, The	■		■									-ick, -urse	In, the, said, with			25
Little Bo-Peep	■		■										in, the, them			26
Little Boy Blue	■		■	■	■							-orn, -eep	in, the			27
Little Jack Horner	■	■											in, a, and			28
Little Miss Muffet	■	■	■										and, a			29
London Bridge						■		■					is, down, it, up, and, my			30
Mary Had A Little Lamb	■		■	■						■		-ay	It, was			31
Monkeys on the Bed			■										the, on, and	■	one less	51
No Potatoes in the Pot		■										-ot, -ay	in	■	two more	52
O-U-T		■										-at	out, the, you			32
One, Two, Buckle My Shoe								■						■	rote counting	33
Pat-A-Cake	■	■						■				-ake, -an	a, it, me, and			34
Pease Porridge		■										-ot, -old	like, it, in, the, some	■		35
Potatoes in the Pot		■										-ot, -ay		■	two less	52
Polly	■	■			■								the, on			36
Rain, Rain							■					-ay, -ain	go, to			37
Sausages in a Pan		■												■	two less	53
Sing a Song of Sixpence		■	■		■					■		-ing	to, a, the	■		38
Spanish Dancer					■	■		■					do, the	■	twenty +	39
Star Light							■					-ight	I		ordinal number	40
Teddy Bear			■					■				-ound, -ight	the	■		41
Ten in the Bed								■					the, and, over	■	one less	54
Tennessee						■							a, see	■		42
This Little Piggy		■	■					■					the, had, little, home	■	ordinal numbers	43
Three Little Kittens, The		■	■							■			no, you, have			44
Tick Tock			■					■					one, has, a		time	45
To Market		■	■							■		-ig, -og	to, home, a			46
Twinkle, Twinkle				■	■		■									47
Who Took the Cookies?	■	■											who, from, the		less	48

Teacher Notes

This book contains a variety of traditional rhymes including nursery rhymes, jump rope rhymes, and counting rhymes. As you glance through the book, you will fondly recall many of these rhymes because you recited or sang them as a child. Because they are familiar to many children, traditional rhymes are a good place to begin teaching or to review specific elements of your language arts curriculum.

Overview

Here is a collection of traditional rhymes that are predictable, enjoyable and thematically appropriate. Each rhyme is presented in large, readable type for your students. Provided next to each rhyme are the Suggestions for Going Further. These suggestions will help you introduce, teach or review specific elements of your curriculum.

Along with the student rhymes and suggestions, we've provided strips for each rhyme that fit into the Desktop Pocket Chart. Using the rhymes, teaching suggestions, and sentence strips provided, you can create a rich interactive learning environment for your students.

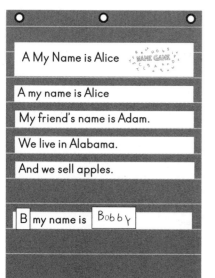

12" wide x 16" high,
10 pockets

What You've Got

- A book of rhymes, at least one for every week of the school year
- Charts that clearly separate the rhymes into themes and skills
- A variety of rhymes: nursery, jump rope, and traditional
- Suggestions on how to develop specific language or mathematics skills
- Suggestions for making the rhymes personal or interactive
- Sentence strips that fit into the Desktop Pocket Chart

The following accessories can be useful when extending the rhymes:

Desktop Pocket Chart

Rhyme of the Week includes strips for each rhyme that fit into the 12" x 16" Desktop Pocket Chart. You can use the strips for activities with individuals or small groups.

Wikki Stix

Made of waxed yarn, Wikki Stix temporarily stick to almost any surface, including the student rhymes and the Desktop Pocket Chart. They provide a visual focus when students are underlining or circling rhyming and number words and other phonemic elements you are teaching.

Highlighter Tape

This removable, colorful, transparent tape can be used to highlight words, phonemic elements, or phrases on the Desktop Pocket Chart.

Sticky Notes

Sticky notes are useful for making rhymes interactive by covering and replacing words on the Desktop Pocket Chart.

Standard Pocket Chart and Sentence Strips

If you choose to, you can write the rhymes on standard pocket chart strips for whole class or small group instruction.

Student Rhymes

For every week of the school year, you have an illustrated rhyme, enlarged for easy reading. You can make a copy of the rhyme for each child, leaving off the Suggestions for Going Further.

Suggestions for Going Further

The suggestions next to the rhymes are activities you can use to extend the rhymes. These suggestions include:

• rhyming word activities
• phonemic element explorations
• creative expression through illustration
• home connection ideas
• ways to make rhymes interactive and personal
• page location of the Desktop Pocket Chart strips

You choose the activities appropriate for your teaching. You may not wish to, or have the time to, complete them all. Feel free to use these suggestions as an idea base from which to create your own activities.

Strips for the Desktop Pocket Chart

The strips lend themselves beautifully to small group work. By copying the strips (starting on page 55) on index tag, cutting them apart, and using them in the Desktop Pocket Chart, you can display a rhyme for all to see. Groups of children can interact with the rhyme using this intimate, yet practical medium.

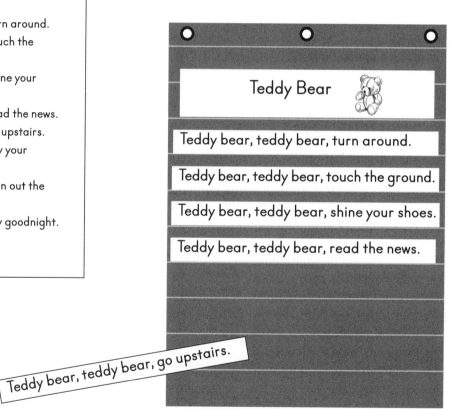

Desktop Strips on pages 87-88

Suggestions for Going Further

1. Have everyone stand in a circle and act out the action of the rhyme.
2. Change the animal name, remembering to stick to three or four syllables to keep the rhythm (e.g., *alligator, alligator; porcupine, porcupine; mountain lion, mountain lion*).
3. Change the activities of the teddy bear:
   Teddy bear, teddy bear, clean your room.
   Teddy bear, teddy bear, use the broom.
   Teddy bear, teddy bear, no t.v.
   Teddy bear, teddy bear, play with me.
   Teddy bear, teddy bear, what do you see?
   Teddy bear, teddy bear, one little bee.
   Teddy bear, teddy bear, touch the sky
   Teddy bear, teddy bear, say goodnight.

Teddy Bear

Teddy bear, teddy bear, turn around.
Teddy bear, teddy bear, touch the ground.
Teddy bear, teddy bear, shine your shoes.
Teddy bear, teddy bear, read the news.
Teddy bear, teddy bear, go upstairs.
Teddy bear, teddy bear, say your prayers.
Teddy bear, teddy bear, turn out the light.
Teddy bear, teddy bear, say goodnight.

41

There are many ways to use *Rhyme of the Week*. You can copy the student rhymes for individual use. You can reconstruct the rhyme in a Desktop Pocket Chart for group work. Or you can make your own strips for a Standard Pocket Chart.

Preparing the Student Rhymes

• Read through and select the rhyme that suits your needs.
• Make a copy of the rhyme without the Suggestions for Going Further for each child in your class.

Ways to Use the Student Rhymes

• Begin to sing a line of one of the rhymes, then stop. Students can sing the missing word or words. For example, you sing, "Twinkle, twinkle little _____" and the children sing, "star."
• Several of the rhymes have actions that traditionally go with the words. Teach the actions whenever possible, since associating actions with words is a great aid to memorization.
• There are many rhymes that lend themselves well to role playing. Acting out the rhymes helps to contextualize the vocabulary for your students.
• Make a copy of the poem without the Suggestions for Going Further and send it home to be shared with family members. See page 9 for other School-Home Connections.
• Make a special rhyme book for each child. Add a new page with every new rhyme you teach. To personalize the books, make sure students illustrate each rhyme, creating meaningful pictures from the words. Reread the books often.
• Ask your librarian to display some of your students' illustrated rhymes, or rhyme books.
• Ask adult volunteers to read rhyming books with individual children in a quiet area.

Going Further with the Student Rhymes

➜ Make the rhymes interactive. Give the children a chance to personalize the rhyme by creating a blank for them to fill in with their own words. It's as simple as whiting out or taping over a word or phrase in the student rhymes before making copies.

➜ Have the children write personalized rhymes:

Baa, Baa, _____ Sheep

Baa, baa, _____ sheep,
Have you any wool?
Yes, sir, yes, sir,
Three bags full;
One for the master,
And one for the dame,
And one for the little boy
Who lives down the lane.

My Name is

D my name is DAANA
My friend's name is JAJ
We live in JoG HoS
And we sell JoLLS

Higglety, Pigglety

Higglety, pigglety, (pop!)
The dog has eaten the (mop;)
The pig's in a (hurry,)
The cat's in a (flurry,)
Higglety, pigglety, (pop!)

← Have the children circle, underline or highlight all the rhyming words.

→ Add new verses or write variations on the rhyme using rhyme frames.

Golden Gate Bridge is shaking now,
shaking now, shaking now.
Golden Gate Bridge is shaking now,
My fair lady.

Build it up with bricks and rocks,
Bricks and rocks, bricks and rocks.
Build it up with bricks and rocks,
My fair lady.

↓ Focus on the mathematics in the rhyme.

Hickory, Dickory, Dock

Hickory, dickory, dock
The mouse went up the clock.
The clock struck _two_ ;
The mouse ran down.
Hickory, dickory, dock

It's Raining

It's raining, it's pouring,
The old man is snoring.
He went to bed
And bumped his head
And couldn't get up in the morning.

← Let children illustrate the rhyme or make a border for it.

→ White out or tape over onsets or rimes in the rhyme, and let the children fill them in.

_ack and _ill

_ack and _ill
Went up the _ill
To fetch a pail of water.
_ack fell _own
And broke his __own,
And _ill came tumbling after.

Preparing the Strips for the Desktop Pocket Chart

- Copy the rhyme strips onto index tag.
- Cut the strips apart.
- Reconstruct the rhyme strips in the Desktop Pocket Chart. We've numbered each line to minimize confusion. You can keep the numbers or cut them off. If a rhyme has more than ten lines, the title and the first line share an enlarged strip.

Ways to Use the Desktop Pocket Chart

- Read the rhyme at a natural speed while the students listen.
- Explain any unfamiliar words and add them to the class word bank.
- Have children listen while you read the rhyme line by line, pointing to each word as you read. Read again and have children repeat while you point. Use one or more student volunteers as pointers while the rest of the group reads.
- While reading, have the children clap their hands to promote greater memorization and to feel the rhythm.
- Point out rhyming words and have students repeat them. Create lists of rhyming words on chart paper that can be placed on a word wall or used as a word bank.
- Promote comprehension by asking students about the characters in the rhyme. For example, questions about Little Miss Muffet could include: Where did Miss Muffet sit? What was she eating? Who came along and scared her away? What would you do if a spider sat next to you?
- Read the list of Suggestions for Going Further that accompanies each rhyme and/or the list that follows for other ideas that reinforce language skills and reinforce other curriculum areas.

Going Further with the Desktop Pocket Chart

- For sorting and sequencing activities, copy the sentence strips and cut them apart. Scramble the strips, and have students put them back in order. Note that each sentence strip is numbered. Cut off the numbers beforehand or include more than one rhyme in your pile of strips.
- Make the rhymes interactive. Give the children a chance to personalize the rhyme by creating a rhyme frame (text with a blank line) for them to fill with their own words. Simply white out or tape over a word or phrase on the strips.
- Have children highlight or underline the particular rhyming word, phrase, or rime you wish to feature.
- Focus on the number words in the counting rhymes.
- Cover phrases in the rhyme with blank strips and let children interact with the rhyme by rewriting the phrases. (Strips for covering should be about 1" high.)
- Let the children use a pointer, such as a star wand, to identify words or letters. See page 10 for the pattern.

- Make lists of rhyming words. Or make webs of words that share a rime or other phonemic element that is emphasized in the rhyme.

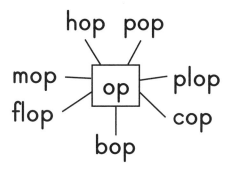

- Use chart paper to create banks of words.

action words

He <u>marched</u> them up the hill

walked

hopped

moved

took

helped

flew

School-Home Connection

- Send home personalized rhyme books once a quarter for students to share with family members and friends.

1. Ask parents or guardians to write comments to their child on the last page of the book about their favorite rhymes and/or how the child "read them." After the comments are written, have students return the books to school for the teacher to read aloud for the class.

2. Be sure to include suggestions for using the rhyme books at home. Suggestions may include:
   - Read orally with the child.
   - Enjoy watching children recite for family members, friends, and favorite stuffed animals.
   - Act out the rhymes using props gathered from around the house.
   - Share in creating illustrations using scrap materials.
   - Help create new verses for the rhymes.
   - Retell one of the rhymes by changing key words as you go.

- Encourage students to bring in and share other rhymes from home. Have the children ask their parents, guardians, grandparents, neighbors or friends if they remember a rhyme from their childhood. Compile a rhyme book for your class library.

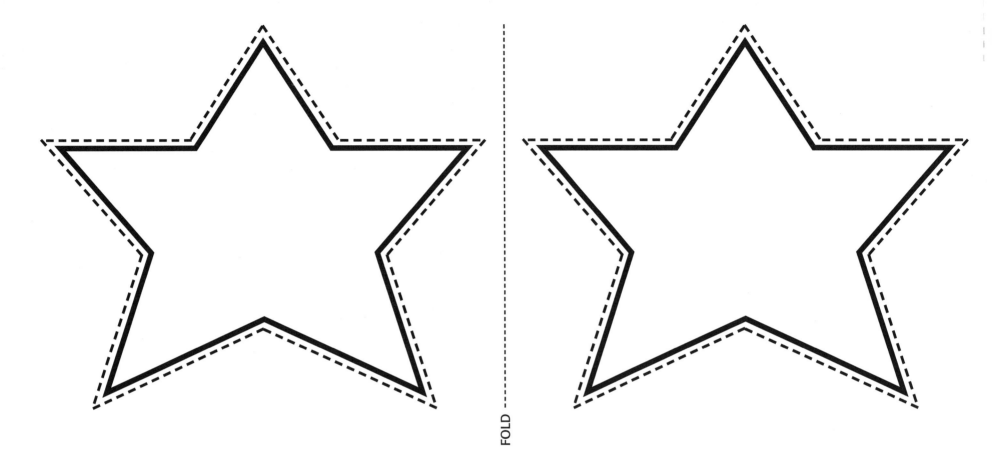

FOLD

Star Wand Pattern
- Copy the stars onto tagboard.
- Fold the stars so they match.
- Staple a plastic straw between the stars.
- Glue the stars together.
- Cut around the stars.
- Decorate the star wand with colored markers, sequins, ribbons and glitter.

Suggestions for Going Further

1. Stand in a circle, clap and jump in place to the rhythm while reciting the rhyme. Have each child take a turn jumping into the center of the circle and personalizing the last sentence. (*K my name is Kathy, X my name is Xavier,* etc.)

2. Make children aware of initial consonants and proper nouns. Ask, "What words in the rhyme begin with capital letters?" Over a period of time, create a version for every letter of the alphabet.

3. Have the children write personalized rhymes. Before making copies of the student rhyme, white out or tape over the words *A, Alice, Adam, Alabama* and *Apples.* Draw lines in place of the covered words. Do the same in the Desktop Pocket Chart using sticky notes or blank strips to cover the replaceable words. Provide the children with copies of the rhyme frame. Have each child fill in the lines with his/her name and other nouns that begin with the first initial of his/her name.

A My Name is Alice

A my name is Alice.

My friend's name is Adam.

We live in Alabama

And we sell apples.

B my name is _____.

Suggestions for Going Further

1. In the Desktop Pocket Chart, cover the word *black* with a sticky note or a blank strip. Have the children use the color words on page 98 and/or the number words on pages 102-103 to change the color of the sheep and/or the number of bags of wool. Have the children create and label an illustration that shows the changes they made in the rhyme.

2. Draw a large sheep on chart paper. Brainstorm things made from wool and write them on the sheep's body (*socks, shirts, coats, gloves,* etc.).

3. Ask students to bring in things from home that are made from wool. Share, label and sort by color and texture.

4. Change the animal in the rhyme, what it sounds like, and what it gives us:
   > *Cluck, cluck, chicken,*
   > *Have you any eggs?*

Baa, Baa, Black Sheep

Baa, baa, black sheep,
Have you any wool?
Yes, sir, yes, sir,
Three bags full;
One for the master,
And one for the dame,
And one for the little boy
Who lives down the lane.

Suggestions for Going Further

1. Have children highlight or underline the rhyming words on their student rhymes. This can also be done on the Desktop Pocket Chart using Wikki Stix or highlighter tape.
2. Discuss all the things (nouns) from the rhyme your students could draw to make a border (*cats, dogs, moon, cows, dishes,* etc.). Have them make borders around their rhymes.
3. Create other nonsense words that rhyme with *fiddle* (*siddle, giddle, hiddle*).
4. Change the animals in the rhyme to tie it in with a farm or zoo unit.
5. Cover the first word in each verse with a sticky note or blank strip, and ask children to recall it. Then try this with the last word in each verse.

The Cat and the Fiddle

Hey diddle, diddle,

The cat and the fiddle,

The cow jumped over the moon.

The little dog laughed

To see such sport,

And the dish ran away

with the spoon.

Suggestions for Going Further

1. Standing in a circle, clap and jump to the rhythm while reciting the rhyme. Practice counting by having each child take a turn saying the next number in order.
2. List all the color words on the board or display the color words from page 98 at the bottom of the chart. Work with the class to find rhyming words for each (e.g., *pink/sink, red/bread, black/pack, blue/shoe, green/cream, brown/town*).
3. Use the color and rhyming words to create new verses.

   Cinderella, dressed in pink,
   Washed her dishes in the kitchen sink.
   How many dishes did she break?
   1, 2, 3, 4...

   Cinderella, dressed in red,
   Went to the store to get some bread.
   How many loaves did she buy?
   1, 2 ,3, 4...

4. Let the children make illustrations to match the new verses. Compile the illustrated verses in a class book.

Cinderella

Cinderella, dressed in yellow,

Went upstairs to kiss a fellow,

Made a mistake and kissed a snake!

How many doctors did it take?

1, 2, 3, 4, 5, 6, 7, 8, 9, 10, 11, 12, 13, 14, 15, 16, 17, 18, 19, 20, 21, 22, 23, 24, 25, 26, 27, 28, 29, 30

Suggestions for Going Further

1. Keep this poem up all year and highlight the months as you go through them.
2. Make a graph while reciting the rhyme, using the blackline on page 99.

Days in the Month	28 or 29 days	30 days	31 days
January			
February			
March			
April			
May			
June			
July			
August			
September			
October			
November			
December			

3. Ask questions to connect the poem to the graph (e.g., How many months have thirty days in them? What is the difference between the days in September and the days in December? How many months are there in one year?).
4. Elicit children's help in showing all the number words in the Desktop Pocket Chart using Wikki Stix or highlighter tape.
5. Discuss the use of capital letters and circle all the initial letters of the months in the rhyme or on the graph.

Days in the Month

Thirty days has September,
April, June, and November;
All the rest have thirty-one,
Except February alone,
And that has twenty-eight
 days clear
And twenty-nine in each
 leap year.

Suggestions for Going Further

1. Have the children march in place as you read the rhyme. See if they can keep up the pace as you vary the speed of your reading. Read the entire rhyme slowly, then read it again at a faster pace.
2. Incorporate body movements as the rhyme is read. Have children stand up tall, then crouch down, then rise up halfway at the appropriate times.
3. Cover the word *march* and brainstorm other action words that can replace it (e.g., *walked, ran, hopped*). Act out the new body movements while reading the newly created verses.
4. Have children be word detectives and highlight the opposites *up* and *down*. Add to your word bank by creating lists of opposites.

The Duke of York

Oh, the brave old Duke of York,

He had ten thousand men.

He marched them up the hill

And marched them down again.

And when they're up, they're up,

And when they're down, they're down,

And when they're only halfway up,

They're neither up nor down.

Suggestions for Going Further

1. Discuss the fact that names begin with capital letters. Have the children change the initial consonants of *Fuzzy* and *Wuzzy* to create new silly names (*Muzzy Nuzzy, Buzzy Duzzy*). The children can also replace the initial consonants of *Fuzzy* and *Wuzzy* with their own first and last initials.
2. Ask, "If Fuzzy Wuzzy wasn't a bear, what animal could he be?"
3. Have the children recite the rhyme as fast as they can.
4. In the Desktop Pocket Chart, cover the first word in each verse with a sticky note or blank strip, and ask children to recall it. Then try this with the last word in each verse.

17

Fuzzy Wuzzy

Fuzzy Wuzzy was a bear.
Fuzzy Wuzzy had no hair.
Fuzzy Wuzzy wasn't very fuzzy,
Was he?

Suggestions for Going Further

1. This rhyme is great for teaching time by the hour. Read it repeatedly, changing *one* to other numbers up to *twelve*. Put a big classroom clock by the Desktop Pocket Chart and have students come up and change the hour on the clock and in the rhyme, using the number words on page 102.
2. Choose one hour of the day (e.g., 7:00 P.M.) and write down activities that children could be doing at that time of day. As a home connection, have students interview someone at home and find out what they might do at that time. Make a graph of the findings.
3. To make the rhyme interactive, have children think of other small animals that could run up the clock. Repeat the rhyme, replacing *mouse* with new words (e.g., *kitten, rat, squirrel*).
4. Cover the word *went* and brainstorm other action words that could replace it (e.g., *walked, jumped, hopped*).

Hickory, Dickory, Dock

Hickory, dickory, dock

The mouse went up the clock.

The clock struck one;

The mouse ran down.

Hickory, dickory, dock

Suggestions for Going Further

1. Distribute copies of the student rhyme and have children find and circle all the rhyming words.
2. Draw a large mop on chart paper and attach words that rhyme with *mop* to the handle. You can add these words to a word wall.
3. Enjoy the silliness of this rhyme by changing the initial consonants in the first verse: (*Bigglety, bigglety, bop! Digglety, digglety, dop!*).
4. You can create a rhyme frame by whiting out or taping over the words *pop, dog, mop, pig,* and *pop* in the student rhyme and replacing them with blank lines before making copies. Do the same in the Desktop Pocket Chart using sticky notes or blank strips. Provide each child with a rhyme frame, and have them fill in new rhyming words and animal words.

Higglety, pigglety, pat!
The moose has eaten the mat;
The sheep's in a hurry,
The cow's in a flurry,
Higglety, pigglety, pat!

Higglety, Pigglety

Higglety, pigglety, pop!
The dog has eaten the mop.
The pig's in a hurry.
The cat's in a flurry.
Higglety, pigglety, pop!

Suggestions for Going Further

1. Sing this song very quietly, as if you don't want to wake up a sleeping baby.
2. Using Wikki Stix or highlighter tape, show all the rhyming words in the Desktop Pocket Chart. Then write the inflection *ing* in the center of a piece of chart paper and brainstorm a web of *ing* words. You may repeat the process with the rime *ay*.

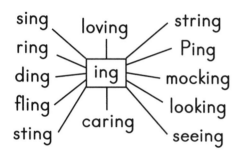

3. Count the number of things Papa is going to buy. Then brainstorm other things Papa could buy.

Hush, Little Baby

Hush, little baby, don't say a word.

Papa's going to buy you a mocking bird.

If that mocking bird won't sing,

Papa's going to buy you a diamond ring.

If that diamond ring turns to brass,

Papa's going to buy you a looking glass.

If that looking glass gets broke,

Papa's going to buy you a billy goat.

If that billy goat runs away,

Papa's going to buy you another today.

Suggestions for Going Further

1. Stand in a circle and clap and jump in place to the rhythm while reciting the rhyme. Practice the alphabet by having each child take a turn saying the next letter in order.
2. Cover the words *ice cream soda* and *Cherry* with sticky notes or blank strips. Brainstorm other foods and their toppings that fit this chant (*Mashed potatoes/Butter on top, Buttermilk pancakes/Syrup on top,* etc.).
3. Create a rhyme frame by whiting out or taping over food words on the student rhyme before making copies. Have students create their own versions using various food words and then illustrate them.

> *Mashed Potatoes*
>
> *Mash potatoes*
> *Butter on top*
> *Who's your friend?*
> *I forgot.*
> *A, B, C, D...*

4. Graph student names by first letter. Draw ice cream cones in a horizontal row on chart paper, labeling each one with a different letter. Draw a scoop for each student name that starts with that letter. Write names on the scoops.

Ice Cream Soda

Ice cream soda
Cherry on top
Who's your friend?
I forgot.
A, B, C, D, E, F, G,
H, I, J, K, L, M, N, O, P,
Q, R, S, T, U, V, W, X, Y, Z

Suggestions for Going Further

1. Brainstorm other small animals that could go up a water spout. Write the animal words (e.g., *bee, ant, moth*) on raindrops made from sticky notes. Cover the word *spider* and have children come up individually and place a raindrop over the blank and recite with the new animal.
2. Make a blackline of large raindrops and distribute copies to the students. Have children write opposites on the raindrops. Cut out, scramble and match the pairs (*up/down, in/out, big/little*, etc.).
3. On chart paper, create lists of things that go up and down (e.g., *elevator, escalator, plane, kite*). Display them on the wall.

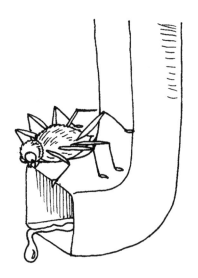

The Itsy, Bitsy Spider

The itsy, bitsy spider
Went up the water spout.
Down came the rain
And washed the spider out.
Out came the sun
And dried up all the rain,
And the itsy, bitsy spider
Went up the spout again.

Suggestions for Going Further

1. Using highlighter tape or Wikki Stix, show the rhyming words (*pouring/snoring/morning* and *bed/head*) in the Desktop Pocket Chart. Brainstorm other words that rhyme with these.
2. Make a simple bed using a shoe box covered with a piece of material. On blank strips or index cards, write other words that rhyme with *bed* and *head* and place them under the "cover." Have individual students pull cards out of the bed, read them aloud, and then stick them on chart paper when finished. Save them for a word bank.
3. Let children illustrate and personalize the poem by drawing themselves in bed, instead of the old man.

It's Raining

It's raining, it's pouring,

The old man is snoring.

He went to bed

And bumped his head

And couldn't get up in the

morning.

Suggestions for Going Further

1. Tape over or white out *Jack* and *Jill* before making copies of the student rhyme. Have each child fill in his/her own name and the name of someone special in the blanks (*Dave* and *Mom* or *Sue* and *Daddy*).
2. Choose pairs of students to act out the rhyme. Give all students an opportunity to "perform." Discuss changing the rhyme by having them break something other than their heads and letting the class decide what they broke.
3. Use chart paper to create banks or webs of words with the rimes *-ill* and *-own* (e.g., *Jill, hill, pill, dill* and *down, crown, clown, town*). Draw a picture of a large pail and write rhyming words inside, or draw a large crown and write rhyming words around the rim.

24

Jack and Jill

Jack and Jill
Went up the hill
To fetch a pail of water.
Jack fell down
And broke his crown,
And Jill came tumbling after.

Suggestions for Going Further

1. Stand in a circle and read the rhyme while clapping the rhythm.
2. Using Wikki Stix or highlighter tape, show the rhyming words (*sick/quick* and *purse/nurse*) in the Desktop Pocket Chart. Brainstorm other words that rhyme with these.
3. Cover the words *doctor* and *nurse* with sticky notes and replace them with other names of people who can help you (e.g., *teacher, plumber, policeman*).
4. Have children cut and divide the strips and use them to act out the poem. Assign parts (doctor, nurse, lady, narrator) and give all students the opportunity to recite lines.
5. Share the book *The Lady With the Alligator Purse* by Natalie Bernard Westcott.

25

The Lady With the Alligator Purse

"Mother, Mother, I am sick.

Send for the doctor quick, quick, quick!"

In came the doctor.

In came the nurse.

In came the lady with the alligator purse.

"Measles," said the doctor.

"Measles," said the nurse.

"Nothing," said the lady

With the alligator purse.

Suggestions for Going Further

1. Discuss ways that Little Bo-Peep could get help in finding her sheep (posters, police station, search party).
2. Discuss the rhyming words (*Peep/sheep*). Before copying the student rhymes, tape over or white out *Bo-Peep* and *sheep* in the title and the first line. Have each child write in his/her own name and something that rhymes with it. Give each student a chance to read his/her new personalized rhyme.
3. Make Little Bo-Peep's staff from tag board. Ask children to search the rhyme for words with the *e* sound. Let students use the staff and point to the words in the Desktop Pocket Chart. To focus on the phoneme, have each child highlight the *e* words (*peep, sheep, leave*) on the student rhyme and then illustrate.
4. Highlight the contraction *they'll*. Discuss the two words that make this contraction. Make a list of other _'ll contractions and the words that make them (*she'll = she+will, he'll = he+will*).

26

Little Bo-Peep

Little Bo-Peep has lost her sheep,
And can't tell where to find them;
Leave them alone, and they'll
   come home,
Wagging their tails behind them.

Suggestions for Going Further

1. Have fun with initial consonants. How many words start with the consonant *b*? Name three words that begin with the consonant *c*. What's the only word that begins with the consonant *m*? Find a word that begins with the consonant *f*.
2. On the Desktop Pocket Chart, use Wikki Stix or highlighter tape to show all the rhyming words.
3. Cover the word *horn* with a sticky note or blank strip. Have the children brainstorm a list of other musical instruments that you can blow (e.g., *trumpet, trombone, tuba*) and use them to replace *horn*. Cover the word *blue* and replace it with other color words. (See page 98.) Do the same with the animal words.
4. Let children answer questions the rhyme raises: What's the name of the little boy? What instrument is he blowing? Where's the sheep? Where's the cow? Where's the little boy? Why is he blowing a horn? What would you do to gather the sheep other than blowing a horn?
5. Cover the word *haystack* and replace it with other places Little Boy Blue could sleep (e.g., *big rock, bed*).

Little Boy Blue

Little Boy Blue, come, blow your horn!
The sheep's in the meadow,
The cow's in the corn.
Where's the little boy
That looks after the sheep?
Under the haystack, fast asleep!

Suggestions for Going Further

1. Before copying the student rhyme, tape over or white out the name *Jack Horner*. Let the students personalize the rhyme by filling in their own first and last names. Have children illustrate the rhyme at the bottom, drawing themselves instead of Jack Horner.
2. To make the rhyme interactive, cover the word *plum* with a sticky note or blank strip. Next to your Desktop Pocket Chart, draw a large pie on chart paper. Brainstorm other fruits (e.g., *peach, cherry, apple*) and write them on the pie.
3. Change the holiday by covering the word *Christmas*. Make a list of other holiday choices on chart paper.
4. Create and illustrate a new rhyme, changing the words *Jack Horner, Christmas* and *plum* (and *He, his,* and *boy,* if necessary).

Little Amy Horner
Sat in a corner
Eating a Passover pie;
She put in her thumb
And pulled out an apple,
And said, "Oh, what a
good girl am I!"

Little Jack Horner

Little Jack Horner
Sat in a corner
Eating a Christmas pie.
He put in his thumb,
And pulled out a plum,
And said, "Oh, what a good
boy am I!"

Suggestions for Going Further

1. Have students identify the pairs of rhyming words in the rhyme.
2. Brainstorm other foods Miss Muffet can eat together. Label a piece of chart paper "Foods We Like to Eat Together" and write down responses (e.g., *beans and franks, hamburger and fries*).
3. Brainstorm other animals that might frighten Miss Muffet. Label a piece of chart paper "Scary Animals" and write down responses (e.g., *lion, bumblebee, mosquito, wasp*).
4. Before copying the student rhymes, white out or tape over any of these words: *Miss Muffet, her, curds, whey* and *spider.* Let the children replace them with their names and appropriate pronouns, foods they like to eat together and/or an animal they think is scary.

29

Little Miss Muffet

Little Miss Muffet
Sat on a tuffet,
Eating her curds and whey.
Along came a spider,
Who sat down beside her
And frightened Miss
     Muffet away.

Suggestions for Going Further

1. Have everyone hold hands and form a big circle. As you recite or sing the first verse, slowly bend forward. As you sing the second verse, slowly straighten up.
2. Focus on the sight words in the rhyme: *is, it, up,* and *my.*
3. Brainstorm other materials the bridge could be built with (e.g., *bricks, concrete, rocks*) and use them in place of sticks and stones:
   Build it up with bricks and rocks,
   Bricks and rocks, bricks and rocks.
   Build it up with bricks and rocks,
   My fair lady.
4. In the student rhymes or the Desktop Pocket Chart, have students underline and count all the words that begin with the letter *s* (eight words). Circle the opposites (*up/down*). Find a word that rhymes with *clown* and put a box around it.
5. Place a blank strip or a sticky note over the word *London*. Ask the students for names of other cities and bridges (e.g., *Buffalo Bridge, Hollywood Bridge, Golden Gate Bridge*).

London Bridge

London Bridge is falling down,
Falling down, falling down.
London Bridge is falling down,
My fair lady.
Build it up with sticks and stones,
Sticks and stones, sticks and
   stones.
Build it up with sticks and stones,
My fair lady.

Desktop Strips on pages 76-77

Suggestions for Going Further

1. Before copying the student rhyme, tape over or white out the name *Mary* whenever it appears, including in the title. Let children personalize the rhyme by writing in their own names.
2. As you read the rhyme in the Desktop Pocket Chart, show the rhyming words using Wikki Stix or highlighter tape. Have the children underline the rhyming words in the student rhymes.
3. Using sticky notes or blank strips, replace the second word in each pair of rhyming words (leave *snow*, cover *go*). Read the rhyme again.
4. Think of things as white as snow (e.g., *cotton*, *clouds*) and use them to replace *snow* in the poem. Then change the color word and brainstorm things that are that color to replace *snow* (*black as coal, brown as wood*, etc.).
5. Let the children rewrite lines 1 and 2 of the rhyme and illustrate. Compile the new lines as a class book.

> *Mary had a little cat,*
> *Its fur was black as coal.*

31

Mary Had A Little Lamb

Mary had a little lamb;

Its fleece was white as snow.

And everywhere that Mary went,

The lamb was sure to go.

It followed her to school one day;

That was against the rules.

It made the children laugh
   and play

To see a lamb at school.

Suggestions for Going Further

1. Let the children change the color of the hat using the color words from page 98. Have one student at a time find the color word you ask for and place it in the rhyme in the Desktop Pocket Chart.
2. Create new verses by replacing the rhyming words *rat/cat/hat*:

   Out goes the man,
   Out goes the can,
   Out goes the lady
   With the big green pan...

3. White out or tape over *rat, cat,* and *hat* on the student rhyme before making copies. Have each child fill in a new set of rhyming words and then illustrate a border around the rhyme.
4. Brainstorm other three-letter words to spell.

O-U-T

Out goes the rat,

Out goes the cat,

Out goes the lady

With the big green hat.

Y-O-U spells you.

O-U-T spells out!

Suggestions for Going Further

1. Students can practice their number word recognition by underlining or highlighting number words on their student copies. Also show number words in the Desktop Pocket Chart using highlighter tape or Wikki Stix.
2. Let individual children say a number word and choose a partner to point to this word in the poem. Provide the children with the number word cards from pages 102-103 and have them match capitalized and lower case number words.
3. Replace the action words to create a new verse:
   One, two, tie my shoe.
   Three, four, open the door.
   Five, six, cut the sticks.
   Seven, eight, stay out late.
   Nine, ten, back again!
4. Make a web using the rime *ick*. Use words from the rhyme and other words (e.g., *sick, sticks, pick, lick, Rick, Dick,*).

One, Two, Buckle My Shoe

One, two, buckle my shoe.
Three, four, shut the door.
Five, six, pick up sticks.
Seven, eight, lay them straight.
Nine, ten, begin again!

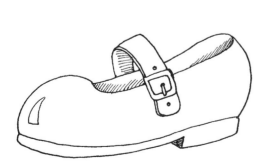

Suggestions for Going Further

1. Have everyone stand and clap their hands to the rhyme while reciting it. Or have pairs of children face each other and clap each other's hands while reciting.

2. Write down students' names on blank strips and copy and cut out their first initials (from page 98). Place them near the rhyme in the Desktop Pocket Chart. Have children place their own initials and names over the letter *T* and the name *Tommy* in the Chart, then read the new verse aloud. You can also white out or tape over *T* and *Tommy* in the student rhyme before making copies. Have the children focus on initial consonant recognition and personalize the rhyme by filling in their own initials and names and illustrating.

3. Brainstorm other foods you can bake in an oven besides cake. Draw a large oven on chart paper and write the words inside. Cover *cake* in the rhyme and reread it using the new vocabulary. Have children draw their own ovens with their favorite baked goods inside.

Pat-A-Cake

Pat-a-cake, pat-a-cake,
  baker's man,
Bake me a cake as fast as
  you can.
Pat it and prick it, and
mark it with a T.
Put it in the oven for Tommy
and me.

Suggestions for Going Further

1. On their student rhymes, have children highlight or underline all the words that begin with the initial consonant *p*.
2. In the Desktop Pocket Chart, let children change the number of days using the number word cards from page 103.
3. Use this rhyme to work with opposites. Ask the children to name the opposites (*hot/cold, old/new*). Write each pair.
4. On chart paper, create banks of words dealing with the rime *-old* (*cold, old, told, sold*), and the rime *-ot* (*hot, pot, lot*).
5. Brainstorm other kinds of porridge (soup) let the children illustrate their favorite kinds.

Pease Porridge

Pease porridge hot,
Pease porridge cold,
Pease porridge in the pot,
Nine days old.
Some like it hot,
Some like it cold,
Some like it in the pot,
Nine days old.

Suggestions for Going Further

1. White out or tape over the name *Polly* in the student rhyme before making copies. Children can easily personalize this rhyme by writing in their own names.
2. Replace the word *muffin* with other favorite sweets. Graph the answers.
3. Replace the word *tea* with hot drinks. Graph the answers.

Polly

Polly put the kettle on,
Polly put the kettle on,
Polly put the kettle on,
We'll all have tea.

Polly put the kettle on,
Sally blow the bellows strong,
Molly call the muffin man,
We'll all have tea.

Suggestions for Going Further

1. White out or tape over the name *Johnny* before copying the student rhymes. Children can easily personalize this rhyme by writing in their own names.
2. Have the children find all the words in the rhyme that end with *ay*. Then they can try to find other *ay* words.
3. Brainstorm other kinds of weather (e.g., *snow, hail, heat*). Repeat the rhyme, replacing *rain*.

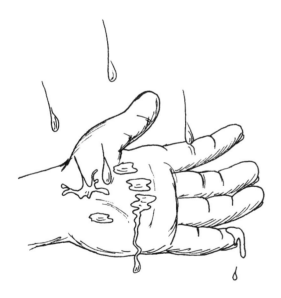

Rain, Rain

Rain, rain, go away,
Come again another day.
Little Johnny wants to play.
Rain, rain, go to Spain,
Never show your face again.

Suggestions for Going Further

1. Draw a large pie on chart paper. Write pairs of rhyming words in the pie.
2. Play around with changing the rhyme. Cover the word *pie* with a sticky note or blank strip. Brainstorm kinds of baked goods. Cover the word *birds* and think of other kinds of birds that could begin to sing (e.g., *robin, bluebird, cardinal*). Talk about why this dish might be for someone other than a king.
3. Use the number word cards from pages 102-103 to replace the words *Four* and *twenty* (*three and thirty, Five and forty*). Using manipulatives and/or illustrations, have the children figure out what the number words represent.

Sing a Song of Sixpence

Sing a song of sixpence,
A pocket full of rye;
Four and twenty blackbirds
Baked in a pie.
When the pie was opened,
The birds began to sing.
Wasn't that a dainty dish
To set before a king?

Suggestions for Going Further

1. Stand in a circle and act out the actions of the rhyme.
2. Substitute different nationalities to replace *Spanish* (*English, French, Mexican, Chinese,* etc.).
3. Have students highlight the sight word *the* on their student rhymes.
4. Create a list of physical activities occurring in the rhyme (splits, kicks, doing rounds, touching the ground). Add the children's suggestions to the list.
5. To make this poem interactive, cover up the last line, *Get out of town*. Make up new lines using words that rhyme with *ground*. (e.g., *Go lie down*, or *Don't make a sound*).

Spanish Dancer

Spanish dancer,
Do the splits.
Spanish dancer,
Do high kicks.
Spanish dancer,
Do the rounds.
Spanish dancer,
Touch the ground.
Spanish dancer,
Get out of town.

Suggestions for Going Further

1. In the Desktop Pocket Chart, show all the *ight* words using Wikki Stix or highlighter tape.
2. Discuss wishes, then help the children write their wishes on stars, using the pattern from page 100. Let the children make the stars more decorative by gluing glitter all around them.
3. Make a magic wand with a star at the top, using the blacklines provided on page 10. Then let students use it to point to the rhyming words with the long *i* pattern *ight*.

Star Light

Star light, star bright,
First star I see tonight,
I wish I may, I wish I might
Have the wish I wish tonight.

Suggestions for Going Further

1. Have everyone stand in a circle and act out the action of the rhyme.
2. Change the animal name, remembering to stick to three or four syllables to keep the rhythm (e.g., *alligator, alligator; porcupine, porcupine; mountain lion, mountain lion*).
3. Change the activities of the teddy bear:
   Teddy bear, teddy bear, clean your room.
   Teddy bear, teddy bear, use the broom.
   Teddy bear, teddy bear, no t.v.
   Teddy bear, teddy bear, play with me.
   Teddy bear, teddy bear, what do you see?
   Teddy bear, teddy bear, one little bee.
   Teddy bear, teddy bear, touch the sky.
   Teddy bear, teddy bear, say goodnight.

41

Teddy Bear

Teddy bear, teddy bear, turn around.

Teddy bear, teddy bear, touch the ground.

Teddy bear, teddy bear, shine your shoes.

Teddy bear, teddy bear, read the news.

Teddy bear, teddy bear, go upstairs.

Teddy bear, teddy bear, say your prayers.

Teddy bear, teddy bear, turn out the light.

Teddy bear, teddy bear, say goodnight.

Suggestions for Going Further

1. Use Wikki Stix or highlighter tape to show the number words in the rhyme in the Desktop Pocket Chart.
2. Have children cut copies of the rhyme into strips, then turn them over and mix them up. Then have them turn the strips front-side up and put them in order.
3. On the rhyme strips, write the corresponding numerals to match the number words.
4. Use poetry strips to make number sentences:
   Four = a-see + two = a-see = _____.
   Nine = a-see − seven-a-see = _____.

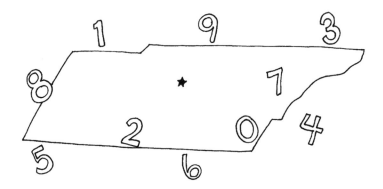

Tennessee

This is the way you spell Tennessee:

One-a-see

Two-a-see

Three-a-see

Four-a-see

Five-a-see

Six-a-see

Seven-a-see

Eight-a-see

Nine-a-see

Tennessee!

Suggestions for Going Further

1. Act out the rhyme by wiggling your fingers, starting with the thumb.
2. Add a new verse or two using suggestions generated by students. Make a list of stores, places, foods, and events that are suitable to your geographical area and title it "What's Special About My Neighborhood." You can save the list for a word bank. Rewrite the rhyme collectively, using new words from the chart.

   The first little piggy went to the Giants
   baseball game.
   The second little piggy stayed home.
   The third little piggy had Ghirardelli chocolate.
   The fourth little pig had none.
   The fifth little piggy cried, "Bye, bye, bye!"
   All the way home.

3. Mix up the strips and let the children place them in order again.

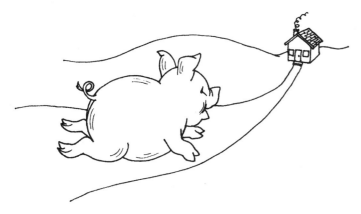

43

This Little Piggy

The first little piggy went to the market.

The second little piggy stayed home.

The third little piggy had roast beef.

The fourth little piggy had none.

The fifth little piggy cried, "Wee, wee, wee!"

All the way home.

Suggestions for Going Further

1. Let children act out this rhyme using paper mittens as props. Then provide each child with a piece of paper folded into thirds. Have them use the first section to show what happened in the beginning of the story, the second section to show the middle of the story and the third section to show the end of the story.

2. Change the animal and the lost object in the first two verses (e.g., *cats/baseball bats, bears/underwear, ducks/toy trucks*).

3. Let the children create borders around the student rhyme on their copies.

4. Divide the class in half. Have one half illustrate their rhymes showing the kittens and how they feel about losing their mittens and being scolded. The rest of the students can illustrate the mother kitten and how she feels.

5. This rhyme is great for choral reading (i.e., a narrator says the first three lines, half the class recites the lines of the kittens and the other half recites the lines of the mother).

6. Brainstorm what might happen if the kittens *found* their mittens.

The Three Little Kittens

The three little kittens
Lost their mittens,
And they began to cry,
"Oh, Mother dear,
We sadly fear
Our mittens we have lost."
"What? Lost your mittens?
You naughty kittens!
Then you shall have no pie."
"Mee-ow, mee-ow, mee-ow!"
"No, you shall have no pie."

Suggestions for Going Further

1. Standing in a circle, clap and jump while reciting the rhyme. Provide each child with an alphabet card from page 98, then continue the rhyme and complete the alphabet by having each child say a word for the letter card they are holding.

   One has an elephant,
   One has a fig,
   One has a goat, . . .

2. Change the time using the number words provided on page 103, (*Ten o'clock, Two o'clock*). Use a classroom clock to demonstrate.

3. Make a blackline with the sentence frame *"One has a(an)_____,"* written across the bottom. Make student copies and have each child illustrate a word for one letter of the alphabet and write the illustrated word on the blank space. Make a big book of these illustrated lines to share.

Tick Tock

Tick tock, tick tock.

Nine o'clock is striking.

Mother, may I go out?

All the kids are waiting.

One has an apple,

One has a bear,

One has a cookie,

One has a dollar,

One has a _____.

Desktop Strips on pages 94-95

Suggestions for Going Further

1. To make the rhyme interactive, cover the word *plum* in the rhyme strips. On chart paper, make a list of different fruits to bring home (*cherry, peach*). Have students choose their favorite fruits and write them on blank strips. Use their strips when re-reading the rhyme.
2. Add a new verse, changing what you will buy and where you buy it from:
   To Bakery
   To bakery, to bakery, to buy a white cake,
   Home again, home again, jiggety jake.
3. Illustrate what the market might look like. Include all the kinds of food you might find there.

To Market

To market, to market, to buy a fat pig,

Home again, home again, jiggety jig.

To market, to market, to buy a fat hog,

Home again, home again, jiggety jog.

To market, to market, to buy a

   plum bun,

Home again, home again, market

   is done.

Suggestions for Going Further

1. Let children use a pointer and point to the rhyming words in the rhyme in the Desktop Pocket Chart.
2. Use hand movements to illustrate the poem as you read it aloud. Allow children freedom to invent their own movements while reading.
3. Brainstorm other words for *twinkle* (e.g., *glitter, sparkle, shine*). Reread with the new words.
4. For a science connection, discuss day/night and why we only see the stars at night.
5. Use the rhyme below to reinforce math skills. Place these strips and any number of stars in the Desktop Pocket Chart.

    Twinkle, twinkle, little star,
    Count how many stars there are.

    Have the children count the stars. Then have them make up equations with the numeral cards from page 96. Let them use the stars to represent or solve their equations.

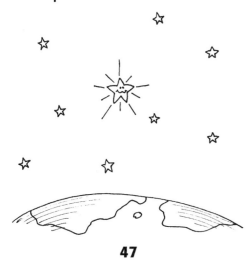

Twinkle, Twinkle

Twinkle, twinkle, little star,
How I wonder what you are!
Up above the world so high,
Like a diamond in the sky.

Suggestions for Going Further

1. Have your students fill in names to personalize the poem.
2. In the Desktop Pocket Chart, use a blank strip or sticky note to cover the word *cookies.* On chart paper, brainstorm different sweets that could be found in a jar to replace it (e.g., *brownies, gummies, peanuts, chocolate*).
3. Let children draw a jar filled with sweets. Then have them write down how many sweets are in the jar.
4. For a math activity, fill up a jar with cookies or candy and have the children become "guesstimators." After everyone estimates the amount, count and enjoy. (Make sure you start with enough for the entire class.)

Who Took the Cookies?

Who took the cookies
From the cookie jar?
_____ took the cookies
From the cookie jar!
Who, me?
Yes, you!
Couldn't be!
Then who?

Suggestions for Going Further

1. Play this as a circle game. Select one child to stand alone, then chant or sing the first verse. Select a second child to hold hands with the first child, starting a circle. Then chant, "Two elephants went out to play . . . ." As you read each verse, add another child to the circle until all children are included. Repeat, counting backwards until only one elephant remains.

2. To get the rhyme strips ready in the Desktop Pocket Chart, copy and cut apart the number word cards (up to the highest number you want to explore) on pages 102-103 and the *He* and *They* cards from the rhyme strip pages. Place the capitalized number word cards in order behind the word *One* in the first line of the verse. Place the *elephants* word card behind *elephant* in the first line and the two *They* cards behind *She* in the last two lines. After reciting the first verse, switch the number word and change the pronoun *she* to *they* to recite the next verse.

3. Ask some "what if" questions such as: What if one elephant wanted three more elephants to come and play? How many elephants would there be? Can you write a number sentence to show this? $(1+3=4)$ What if there were four elephants playing and one had to go home? What if four elephants were playing and three had to go home?

Elephants on a Web

<u>One</u> elephant went out to play
Upon a spider's web one day.
She had such enormous fun,
She called for one
other elephant to come.

Repeat, increasing the number of elephants.

Suggestions for Going Further

1. To get the rhyme strips ready in the Desktop Pocket Chart, copy upper and lower case number word cards (up to the highest number you want to explore) on pages 102-103. Cut them apart and place them in descending order behind the number word *Five* in the first line and *four* in the last line. After reciting the first verse, change the number words and recite again.

2. Have children create hand and body motions to accompany the rhyme. Act it out accordingly.

3. Increase the number of frogs on the log and the number that jump into the pool, and have the children illustrate the outcome.

   Fifteen little speckled frogs
   sat on a speckled log
   Eating the most delicious bugs:
   Yum, yum!
   Five jumped into the pool,
   where it was nice and cool,
   Now there are _____
   speckled frogs: Glub, glub!

4. On chart paper, make a list of other words you could use to describe the frog (*bumpy frogs on a bumpy log, slippery frogs on a slippery log*).

Five Speckled Frogs

<u>Five</u> little speckled frogs
sat on a speckled log
Eating the most delicious bugs:
Yum, yum!
One   jumped into the pool,
where it was nice and cool,
Now there are <u>four</u>
speckled frogs: Glub, glub!

Suggestions for Going Further

1. To get the rhyme strips ready in the Desktop Pocket Chart, copy the capitalized number word cards (up to the highest number you want to explore) on page 103. Cut them apart and place them in descending order behind the number word *Five*. After reciting the first verse, change the number word and recite again.

2. Aid memorization by acting out the rhyme with the children: move your fingers up and down to represent jumping, bump your head with your hand to show *bumped*, pretend to hold a phone to call the doctor, and shake your head from side to side while saying the last verse.

3. Have "ten little monkeys" (students) stand in a row. As you recite each verse, replace the number word cards starting with *Ten* (*Nine, Eight,* etc.). As the second line is recited, have one student sit down until there are no "monkeys" left.

4. Cover the word *monkey* in the rhyme. Brainstorm other animals to replace it.

5. Talk about the special marks that are used when someone is talking (" ").

Monkeys on the Bed

Five   little monkeys
jumping on the bed,
One   fell off
and bumped his head.
Mother called the doctor,
and the doctor said,
"No more monkeys
jumping on the bed!"

Repeat, decreasing the number of monkeys.

Suggestions for Going Further

1. To get the rhyme strips ready in the Desktop Pocket Chart, copy the lowercase even number word cards on page 102 and the capitalized even number word cards on page 103 (up to the highest numbers you want to explore). Cut them apart and place the capitalized number words in ascending order behind the word *No* and the lowercase number words in ascending order behind each *two*. After reciting the first verse, change the number words and recite again:

   Potatoes in a pot,
   Put two in and four stay hot.

2. Write the corresponding number equation for each verse $(0 + 2 = 2, 2 + 2 = 4, \ldots)$. Then start over with a higher number and write the number equation for each verse.

   Fourteen potatoes in a pot,
   Put two in and sixteen stay hot.
   $14 + 2 = 16$

3. Recite the rhyme in reverse order to practice subtraction. Use the second set of strips on page 108. Write a corresponding number equation for each verse.

   Ten potatoes in a pot,
   Take two out and eight stay hot.

No Potatoes in the Pot

No___ potatoes in the pot,
Put two in and two stay hot.

Potatoes in a Pot

Ten_ potatoes in a pot,
Take two out and eight stay hot.

Suggestions for Going Further

1. To get the rhyme strips ready in the Desktop Pocket Chart, copy the capitalized number word cards (up to the highest number you want to explore) on page 103. Cut them apart and place the even number words in descending order behind the number word *Ten* in the first line. After reciting the first verse, change the number word to *Eight* and recite again, and so on.

2. Start with an odd number of sausages, and ask the children how many sausages are left when one goes "pop" and another goes "bam".

3. Explore a different number pattern. Begin with an odd number and write the corresponding number equations for each verse.

   Nine fat sausages sitting in a pan,
   One went "pop" and the other went "bam!"
   $9 - 2 = 7$

Sausages in a Pan

Ten fat sausages

sitting in a pan,

One went "pop"

and another went "bam!"

Suggestions for Going Further

1. To get the rhyme strips ready in the Desktop Pocket Chart, copy the upper case number word cards (up to the highest number you want to explore) on page 103. Cut them apart and place them in descending order behind the number word *Ten* in the first line. After reciting the first verse, change the number word and recite again.
2. Act out the rhyme using hand motions to show the "roll over" part.
3. Draw a large bed on chart paper. Generate a list of ideas about the identity of the ten things in the bed (*bugs, bears, children, ants,* etc.). Draw ten "bugs" in bed. While reading the rhyme, use sticky notes to cover each "bug" to show that it has fallen out of the bed. Create number sentences to correspond with each verse (10 − 1 = 9, etc.).
4. Brainstorm other places the ten "bugs" could be besides the bed (*car, jar, tree,* etc.).

Ten in the Bed

Ten in the bed,
and the little one said,
"Roll over! Roll over!"
They all rolled over
and one fell out.

Repeat, decreasing the number down to one, then say the last verse:

One in the bed
and the little one said,
"Alone at last."

Rhyme Strip Table of Contents

1. A My Name is Alice

NAME GAME

2. A my name is Alice.

3. My friend's name is Adam.

4. We live in Alabama

5. And we sell apples.

6. B my name is _____.

Baa, Baa, Black Sheep

Baa, baa, black sheep,

Have you any wool?

Yes, sir, yes, sir,

Three bags full;

One for the master,

And one for the dame,

And one for the little boy

Who lives down the lane.

1

The Cat and the Fiddle

2 Hey diddle, diddle,

3 The cat and the fiddle,

4 The cow jumped over the moon.

5 The little dog laughed

To see such sport,

And the dish ran away with the spoon.

Cinderella

Cinderella, dressed in yellow ,

Went upstairs to kiss a fellow,

Made a mistake and kissed a snake!

How many doctors did it take ?

1, 2, 3, 4, 5, 6, 7, 8, 9, 10, 11, 12,

13, 14, 15, 16, 17, 18, 19, 20, 21,

22, 23, 24, 25, 26, 27, 28, 29, 30

Days in the Month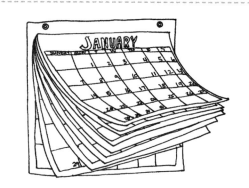

Thirty days has September,

April, June, and November;

All the rest have thirty-one,

Except February alone,

And that has twenty-eight days clear

And twenty-nine in each leap year.

The Duke of York

Oh, the brave old Duke of York,

He had ten thousand men.

He marched them up the hill

And marched them down again.

And when they're up, they're up,

And when they're down, they're down

And when they're only halfway up,

They're neither up nor down.

1

Fuzzy Wuzzy

2

Fuzzy Wuzzy was a bear.

Fuzzy Wuzzy had no hair.

Fuzzy Wuzzy wasn't very fuzzy,

Was he?

Hickory, Dickory, Dock

Hickory, dickory, dock

The mouse went up the clock.

The clock struck one;

The mouse ran down.

Hickory, dickory, dock

1 Higglety, Pigglety

2 Higglety, pigglety, pop!

3 The dog has eaten the mop.

4 The pig's in a hurry.

5 The cat's in a flurry.

Higglety, pigglety, pop!

Hush, Little Baby

Hush, little baby, don't say a word.

Papa's going to buy you a mocking bird.

If that mocking bird won't sing,

Papa's going to buy you a diamond ring.

If that diamond ring turns to brass,

Papa's going to buy you a looking glass.

⁸ If that looking glass gets broke,

⁹ Papa's going to buy you a billy goat.

¹⁰ If that billy goat runs away,

¹¹ Papa's going to buy you another today.

¹ Ice Cream Soda

² Ice cream soda

³ Cherry on top

Who's your friend?

I forgot.

A, B, C, D, E, F, G, H, I, J, K, L, M,

N, O, P, Q, R, S, T, U, V, W, X, Y, Z

The Itsy, Bitsy Spider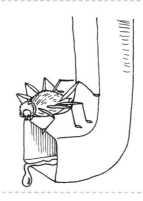

The itsy, bitsy spider

Went up the water spout.

4 Down came the rain

5 And washed the spider out.

6 Out came the sun

7 And dried up all the rain,

8 And the itsy, bitsy spider

9 Went up the spout again.

I It's Raining

Send for the doctor quick, quick, quick!"

In came the doctor.

In came the nurse.

In came the lady with the alligator purse.

"Measles," said the doctor.

"Measles," said the nurse.

"Nothing," said the lady

With the alligator purse.

Little Bo-Peep

Little Bo-Peep has lost her sheep,

And can't tell where to find them;

Leave them alone, and they'll come home,

Wagging their tails behind them.

Little Boy Blue

Little Boy Blue, come, blow your horn!

The sheep's in the meadow,

The cow's in the corn.

Where's the little boy

That looks after the sheep?

Under the haystack, fast asleep!

Little Jack Horner

2 Little Jack Horner

3 Sat in a corner

4 Eating a Christmas pie.

5 He put in his thumb,

6 And pulled out a plum,

7 And said, "Oh, what a good boy am I!"

1
Little Miss Muffet

Little Miss Muffet

Sat on a tuffet,

Eating her curds and whey.

Along came a spider,

Who sat down beside her

And frightened Miss Muffet away.

London Bridge

London Bridge is falling down,

Falling down, falling down.

London Bridge is falling down,

My fair lady.

Build it up with sticks and stones,

Sticks and stones, sticks and stones.

Build it up with sticks and stones,

My fair lady.

Mary Had A Little Lamb

Mary had a little lamb;

Its fleece was white as snow.

And everywhere that Mary went,

The lamb was sure to go.

It followed her to school one day;

That was against the rules.

8 It made the children laugh and play

9 To see a lamb at school.

1

O-U-T

2 Out goes the rat,

3 Out goes the cat,

4 Out goes the lady

5 With the big green hat.

Y-O-U spells you.

O-U-T spells out!

One, Two, Buckle My Shoe

One, two, buckle my shoe.

Three, four, shut the door.

Five, six, pick up sticks.

Seven, eight, lay them straight.

Nine, ten, begin again!

Pat - A - Cake

2 Pat-a-cake, pat-a-cake, baker's man,

3 Bake me a cake as fast as you can.

4 Pat it and prick it, and mark it with a <u>T</u>.

5 Put it in the oven for <u>Tommy</u> and me.

Pease Porridge

Pease porridge hot,

Pease porridge cold,

Pease porridge in the pot,

Nine days old.

Some like it hot,

Some like it cold,

8

Some like it in the pot,

Nine days old.

1

Polly

2 Polly put the kettle on,

3 Polly put the kettle on,

4 Polly put the kettle on,

5 We'll all have tea.

Polly put the kettle on,

Sally blow the bellows strong,

Molly call the muffin man,

We'll all have tea.

Rain, Rain

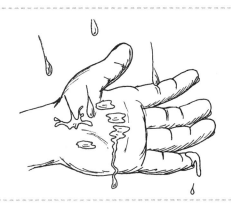

Rain, rain, go away,

Come again another day.

4 Little Johnny wants to play.

5 Rain, rain, go to Spain,

6 Never show your face again.

1 Sing a Song of Sixpence

2 Sing a song of sixpence,

3 A pocket full of rye;

4 Four and twenty blackbirds

5 Baked in a pie.

6 When the pie was opened,

7 The birds began to sing.

8 Wasn't that a dainty dish

9 To set before a king?

1   Spanish Dancer

2 Spanish dancer,

3 Do the splits.

4 Spanish dancer,

5 Do high kicks.

6 Spanish dancer,

7 Do the rounds.

8 Spanish dancer,

9 Touch the ground.

10 Spanish dancer,

11 Get out of town.

Star Light

Star light, star bright,

First star I see tonight,

I wish I may, I wish I might

Have the wish I wish tonight.

Teddy Bear

2 Teddy bear, teddy bear, turn around.

3 Teddy bear, teddy bear, touch the ground

4 Teddy bear, teddy bear, shine your shoes.

5 Teddy bear, teddy bear, read the news.

6 Teddy bear, teddy bear, go upstairs.

7 Teddy bear, teddy bear, say your prayers.

8 Teddy bear, teddy bear, turn out the light.

9 Teddy bear, teddy bear, say goodnight.

Tennessee

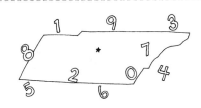

This is the way you spell Tennessee:

One - a - see

Two - a - see

Three - a - see

Four - a - see

Five - a - see

Six - a - see

⁹ Seven - a - see

¹⁰ Eight - a - see

¹¹ Nine - a - see, Tennessee!

¹ This Little Piggy

² The first little piggy went to the market.

³ The second little piggy stayed home.

The third little piggy had roast beef.

The fourth little piggy had none.

The fifth little piggy cried, "Wee, wee, wee!"

All the way home.

The three little kittens
Lost their mittens,

And they began to cry,

"Oh, Mother dear,

5 We sadly fear

6 Our mittens we have lost."

7 "What? Lost your mittens?

8 You naughty kittens!

9 Then you shall have no pie."

10 "Mee-ow, mee-ow, mee-ow!"

11 "No, you shall have no pie."

Tick Tock

Tick tock, tick tock.

Nine o'clock is striking.

Mother, may I go out?

All the kids are waiting.

One has an apple,

One has a bear,

⁸ One has a cookie,

⁹ One has a dollar,

¹⁰ One has a _____ .

¹ To Market

² To market, to market, to buy a fat pig,

³ Home again , home again, jiggety jig.

⁴ To market, to market, to buy a fat hog,

5 Home again, home again, jiggety jog.

6 To market, to market, to buy a plum bun,

7 Home again, home again, market is done.

Twinkle, Twinkle

2 Twinkle, twinkle, little star,

3 How I wonder what you are!

4 Up above the world so high,

Like a diamond in the sky.

Count how many stars there are.

| 1 | 2 | 3 | 4 | 5 | 6 | 7 | 8 | 9 | 10 | 11 |

| 12 | 13 | 14 | 15 | 16 | 17 | 18 | 19 | 20 | 21 | 22 |

23 24 25 26 27 28 29 30 + =

☆ ☆ ☆ ☆ ☆ ☆ ☆ ☆ ☆ ☆

☆ ☆ ☆ ☆ ☆ ☆ ☆ ☆ ☆ ☆

☆ ☆ ☆ ☆ ☆ ☆ ☆ ☆ ☆ ☆

Who Took the Cookies?

Who took the cookies

From the cookie jar?

___Anne___ took the cookies

From the cookie jar!

Who, me?

Yes, you!

8 Couldn't be!

9 Then who?

A B C D E F G H I J K
L M N O P Q R S T U V
W X Y Z

red   orange   yellow   green

blue   purple   black   brown

tan   pink   white   gray

Days in the Month	28 or 29 days	30 days	31 days
January			
February			
March			
April			
May			
June			
July			
August			
September			
October			
November			
December			

Counting Rhymes

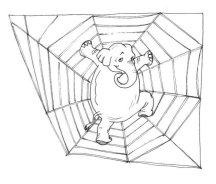

The counting rhyme strips in the following section work with the number word cards, so that you can increase or decrease the numbers while reciting the verses. (There are extra words provided for having a greater number added or subtracted.)

1. To get the strips ready for the Desktop Pocket Chart, copy the number word cards, pages 102-103, as explained in the Suggestions for Going Further for that rhyme (see pages 49-54.)
2. Copy and cut apart the cards. Place them directly behind the underlined words they are intended to cover.
3. After reciting the first verse, change the number word(s) and any other word(s) as suggested. Then recite the verse with the changed words.
4. We have also included a few extra words so you can change the parts of the rhyme that control the number of characters that join or depart. Consider:
   calling more than one elephant to come,
   having more than one frog jump into the pond,
   having more than one monkey bump his head,
   having more than one sausage "pop" and "bam",
   or having more than one fall out of bed.

one	two	three	four	five
. 1	.. 2	... 3	:: 4	:: 5

six	seven	eight	nine	ten
::: 6	::.. 7	::::: 8	::::: 9	:::: 10

eleven twelve thirteen fourteen

fifteen sixteen seventeen eighteen

nineteen

ten	twenty	thirty	forty

fifty	sixty	seventy	eighty

ninety

One Two Three Four Five

1 2 3 4 5

Six Seven Eight Nine Ten

6 7 8 9 10

Eleven Twelve Thirteen Fourteen

Fifteen Sixteen Seventeen

Eighteen Nineteen

Ten Twenty Thirty Forty

Fifty Sixty Seventy Eighty

Ninety

Elephants on a Web

 __One__ __elephant__ went out to play

Upon a spider's web one day.

__She__ had such enormous fun,

__She__ called for one

other elephant to come. He He

elephants elephants They They

Five Speckled Frogs

 <u>Five</u> little speckled frogs

sat on a speckled log

Eating the most delicious bugs:

Yum, yum!

One jumped into the pool,

where it was nice and cool.

Now there are <u>four</u>

speckled frogs: Glub, glub!

frog frog   is

Monkeys on the Bed

<u>Five</u> little monkeys

jumping on the bed,

One   fell off

and bumped __his__ head.

Mother called the doctor,

and the doctor said,

"No more monkeys

jumping on the bed!"

monkey their heads.

No Potatoes in the Pot

² <u>No</u> potatoes in the pot,

³ Put two in and <u>two</u> stay hot.

¹ Potatoes in the Pot

² <u>Ten</u> potatoes in the pot,

³ Take two out and <u>eight</u> stay hot

¹ Sausages in a Pan

108

<u>Ten</u> fat sausages

sitting in a pan,

One went "pop"

and another went "bam!"

Ten in the Bed

<u>Ten</u> in the bed

and the little one said,

4 "Roll over! Roll over!"

5 They all rolled over

6 and one fell out.

7 "Alone at last."